THE MIRACLE OF ONENESS

A Premarital Guide for Believers

Gregory L. Payton

The Miracle of Oneness Copyright © 2021 by Gregory Payton. All Rights Reserved.

All rights reserved. No part of this book may be reproduced in any form or by any electronic or mechanical means including information storage and retrieval systems, without permission in writing from the author. The only exception is by a reviewer, who may quote short excerpts in a review.

The Holy Bible, New International Version®, NIV® Copyright © 1973, 1978, 1984, 2011 by Biblica, Inc.® Used by permission. All rights reserved worldwide.

Cover designed by AviLuxe Designs

Please visit the author's website:
www.miracleofoneness.com

Printed in the United States of America

First Printing: March 2021
The Scribe Tribe Publishing Group

ISBN-978-1-7358251-2-0 (print)
ISBN-978-1-7358251-3-7 (electronic)

This book is dedicated to my parents, Edison and Gwendolyn Payton. My parents were married for 52 years before my father went home to be with the Lord in 2013. I witnessed a beautiful and loving marriage for 47 years of my life. I pray that the information in this book will make them both proud of me as a man of integrity and humility. I learned most of what I know about marriage by observing the two of them as Husband and Wife.

Daddy and Mommy,
I love you both tremendously, and I dedicate this work to the two of you!

Keyonna,

My love, my heart, my dear friend, my prayer partner, my companion, my BROWN SUGAR!

You are so many different things to me, and I am overwhelmed with joy and excitement as I stand here today holding your hands and looking into your eyes.

As I prayed this morning, I thanked God for loving me so much by allowing me to find someone as special as you.

As undeserving as I am, God's grace and His mercy led me to be with someone who loves me in a way that I have never been loved before.

Your smile warms my heart!

Your voice calms my soul.

Your eyes make me feel like someone spectacular when you look at me.

When you walk into a room, I feel like time stops just so I can admire how amazingly beautiful you are.

I thank God for creating a woman that is not only a pleasure to look at but a pleasure to be in the presence of every time I see you.

Your kindness towards me reminds me of how much you simply love me because I am me.

Your courage and your daily effort to do better and to be better has motivated me to do better and to be better.

Your strength and your determination inspire me to be a better man.

You believed in me when I doubted myself.

Your patience with me has helped me strive to be a more patient person.

You touched my heart when it was broken.

You allowed God to use you to help mend my heart when it was broken.

You loved me when I thought no one could see me for who I am.

You have shown me that dreams can come true by having unwavering faith in God.

When you hug me, I am consumed with the warmth of your love for me.

When you talk to me, you help me make it through each day.

When you pray for me and when you pray with me, I am reminded of how much you love me and how much God loves me.

The fact that you once thanked me for praying for you, shows me how humble and gentle your spirit is.
You say 'amen' the loudest when I am preaching a sermon!
You are so beautiful to me!
You are not only physically beautiful, but you are spiritually beautiful.
And I thank and praise God for creating you just for me!
I am the HAPPIEST MAN on the planet because I found a wife that embodies the character traits of the woman described in Proverbs 31.
The Bible says in Proverbs 18:22 that he who finds a wife finds a good thing and obtains favor from the Lord.
I found my wife.
I found not just a good thing, but a great thing!
And I have obtained favor from the Lord!
I promise to give you my heart, my love, and a tremendous effort in being the greatest husband on the earth to you because you deserve it, you're worth it, and because I love you more than you could ever imagine!
Loving you and experiencing the pleasure of having you in my life reminds me of how great God is and how much He loves us all.
I love you Keyonna!

My vows as spoken to my wife on our wedding day, **October 12, 2014.**

CONTENTS

Foreword 3
Introduction 7
Session One 11
Session Two 17
Session Three 23
Session Four 27
Session Five 37
Session Six 49
Final Note 55
Appendix 57
Acknowledgements 63
About the Author 65
Works Cited 67

FOREWORD

Good houses don't just happen, neither do good marriages! That is why what God is doing through Gregory in this book is so amazing. God is providing His divine blueprint and pointing the way of a "biblically" successful marriage.

By wisdom a house is built, and by understanding it is established; by knowledge the rooms are filled with all precious and pleasant riches.
Proverbs 24:3-4

Do you want the rooms of your life and your marriage to be filled with *precious and pleasant riches*? God's word says, *"by knowledge"* that happens. In His word, God has given us the understanding and knowledge we need to build a marriage that is pleasing to Him, not to ourselves. That wisdom means that we follow His plan. The blessing of building a marriage and a home with God's wisdom, God's understanding, and God's knowledge will bring precious and pleasant riches – certainly in the spiritual sense and often in the material sense. God's blessing is on the marriage that seeks and honors His wisdom.

This premarital guide is a perfect blend of biblical and sociological principles that answer the questions – first, what does God say, and then, how do I live that out in the culture that surrounds me everyday life. Gregory has developed a winning strategy by implementing powerful questions that help raise and define real issues that show up in marriages – questions that push one toward framing the right solutions – questions that teach!

Couples planning marriage – this is a high-priority guide for the future success of your marriage. Singles contemplating marriage – it's never too soon to learn the principles shared in this guide. Pastors, mentors, and counselors – you will find the teaching and exercises helpful as you counsel married couples as well as pre-marital couples.

On a personal note, I have known and pastored Gregory and his family since 2017. He and his family are testament to what he teaches in this book. This is a gift of great value for anyone, even those who are not yet considering marriage. So please, buy it, keep a copy in your library, and be intentional to share it with others.

Corey B. Brooks
Senior Pastor, New Beginnings Church of Chicago
CEO, ProjectH.O.O.D. Communities Development Corporation

Gregory L. Payton

Gregory L. Payton

INTRODUCTION

"Haven't you read," he replied, "that at the beginning the Creator 'made them male and female,' and said, 'For this reason a man will leave his father and mother and be united to his wife, and the two will become one flesh'? So, they are no longer two, but one flesh. Therefore; what God has joined together, let no one separate." Matthew 19:4-6 (NIV)

Congratulations! You have chosen to review this study guide because you are considering one of the biggest decisions you will make in your life. The two of you have decided to become husband and wife for the rest of your lives. At this moment, you may be deeply in love with one another. When one of you thinks of the other, your heart begins to flutter, and a smile immediately comes across your face. You probably have hopes and dreams of how your future will be as you embark on this journey called Marriage. Based on what you have observed in your life, you probably have an idea of how you think marriage is or how it should be. Prayerfully, you have had positive influences in your individual lives that have properly modeled marriage before your eyes. Sadly, you may have observed some negative modeling of marriage throughout your life or you may have even allowed the world to give you a carnal presentation of how the marriage relationship should be.

Because of the many thoughts and ideas you may have, I am glad you have decided to seek some help and information prior to committing to marriage. Unfortunately, so many couples have jumped into marriage without any kind of preparation or idea of how a marriage should be. Some of those who are now married would be better off today if they had the benefit of pre-marital counseling. Similarly, there are also some people who may have decided not to marry if they took a good look at what they were about to get themselves into prior to marriage! If only our society would support the idea of a short preparation period for a lifelong investment such as marriage. It is funny that we will spend years in school to secure an education to gain employment for thirty to forty years of our lives before retiring. We can invest nine years of elementary school, four years of high school, four to five years of college, and maybe even two to three years of graduate studies to prepare ourselves for careers that may or may not be fulfilling. When comparing this idea of preparation through education to the idea of three to six months of pre-marital counseling to prepare for a lifetime of marriage, the time spent on counseling may seem too short.

    The fact that you have chosen this study guide shows that you value the institution of marriage. Not only do you value marriage, but you see the importance of preparing for something as valuable as marriage. This guide will give you some biblical principles as well as some sociological principles that will aid you in your marriage. Over the course of the next several months, you will journey through this guide and I will act as your virtual marriage counselor. We will have six "sessions" together. Each session is designed to be completed over a month's time frame, but do not allow this time constraint to discourage you. I am more concerned with you doing the work versus doing it in the allotted time frame. Please take the time to really dive into the lessons and complete the homework assignments. The vitality of your marriage depends on it! This book should not replace the assistance of a qualified biblical counselor; rather it should act as supplemental material as the two of you prepare to embark on the journey of a lifetime. It is imperative to seek out professionals before (and during) marriage who will help you as a couple deal with the issues that will hinder you from having a successful marriage.

    I respectfully ask that you read each lesson thoroughly to be productive throughout this task. Some of the sessions will require extra work and discussions on your part. Please address all the issues and concerns outlined in the lesson to get the maximum educational effect of each session. Please be patient throughout this process and keep in mind that these few weeks are small in comparison to the lifetime that the two of you will be spending together.

Before we go any further, I must emphasize that this guide is written specifically for believers. If one of you has not accepted Christ, we cannot engage in this process. If one of you has not accepted Jesus Christ as your Lord and Savior, I pray that you stop for a second at this very moment and consider accepting Him into your heart. The gift of salvation is available to you now. Marriage must consist of two believers to function properly. If both of you are born again believers, this counseling process is tailor-made just for you. I would ask that you make sure you have a study bible in your possession. I would also ask that you both have open minds and be ready to openly discuss several major issues relating to your marriage.

Our goal here is to help ensure the success of your marriage. It is wise that you have decided to get a solid understanding of marriage now because most couples who neglect this very important step before marriage end up in marriage counseling after they run into difficulties. You will either have counseling now or you will have it later, so it is probably best to get counseling prior to the marriages to avoid major headaches and pain later. The major thought that we must keep in mind is that marriage is an institution that God created. To properly conduct ourselves in marriage, we must understand God's will for marriage. These sessions are designed to help you understand how God expects our marriages to function. The world (the secular society we live in) did not create marriage. Therefore, the world has no right to dictate how marriage should be. The One who created marriage is the One who can show us how to have a happy marriage that brings glory and honor to Him. I pray that God will bless you through these sessions and I pray that your marriage will be one that will bring glory to God as well as much joy and happiness to the two of you for the rest of your lives.

Gregory L. Payton

SESSION ONE

The Biblical Definition of Marriage

Purpose: To give the candidates for marriage a good understanding of how God clearly gives us a definition of marriage as well as His will for marriage through several passages of scripture

What is Marriage? So many of us think we know exactly what marriage is. Some of us have been married for years and we have no clue as to what marriage is. Those of us who are considering marriage think we know what it is even though we have never been married a day in our lives.

The American Heritage Dictionary defines marriage as a legal union of a **man and woman** as husband and wife. This definition sounds good and there is a lot of truth to it. However, marriage is much more than a legal union. One of the key elements of this definition is that marriage involves a man and a woman. It does not involve two men nor does it involve two women. A union of any kind between two people of the same sex is not a marriage. This fact is true whether the definition of marriage be of a secular nature or of a spiritual nature. Marriage is a union between a man and a woman. Let's go a little bit deeper and get a more spiritual definition of marriage.

The Baker Theological Dictionary of the Bible defines marriage as an intimate and complementing union between a man and a woman in which the two become **one** physically, in the whole of life. The purpose of the marriage is to reflect the relationship of the Godhead and to serve Him. Although the fall of man has marred the divine purpose and function of marriage, this definition reflects the God-ordained ideal for marriage from the beginning. (Baker 510) This definition seems good even though it may require that you know a little bit about the Bible and general doctrinal terms. However, the key to this definition again is that it involves a man and a woman.

Relationship or the union between the man and woman is one that is intimate (or close) and beneficial to both partners. **Marriage is to reflect God's relationship towards us.** God loves us unconditionally and He is faithful in His relationship with His people. At this point, I would like for you to read the book of Hosea to get an understanding of how God compares His relationship to Israel with the relationship between the prophet Hosea and his adulterous wife Gomer.

The Bible also uses Christ and His bride, the church, to symbolize the marriage relationship. We will explore this concept later. Overall, we will be looking at various passages of scripture to get an understanding of what marriage is from a biblical perspective. We will also look at several different passages of scripture that will hopefully give us a clear biblical definition of marriage. I will briefly mention the scripture passages with the intent of giving you a general understanding of what they mean and how they are applicable to marriage. The Bible is a tool that God uses in teaching us and guiding us in our lives *(II Timothy 2:16)*

Your assignment after reading through this session of the study guide is to go back and read these passages of scripture together to help each other have a clear understanding of what they mean and how they relate to marriage. After reading the passages together, have a brief discussion on what these passages convey to you and how they will come into play in your marriage. If at some point you completely disagree with what the scripture mandates, prayerfully consider whether marriage is something you are ready to engage in. Hopefully, you can relate the scriptures to how they will benefit the uniqueness of your relationship. I will list detailed instructions for you at the end of this written section.

In the New International Version of the Bible, the word *marriage* is mentioned 43 times. The word *married* is mentioned 78 times, and the word *marry* is mentioned 49 times. For the sake of time, we are not going to explore 170 different uses of words relating to marriage in the Bible. We will mainly focus on a few familiar passages of scripture that I believe will give an understanding of what the Bible says about marriage.

Let's look at Chapter 2 of Genesis. After God created the first man (Adam), he gave him the responsibility of taking care of the Garden of Eden. In verse 18 of this chapter, God realized how much of a responsibility Adam had, so he decided to create a helper for Adam. None of the creatures God created were suitable helpers for him, so God decided to create woman (v. 21-23). Therefore, the first married couple was formed and verse 24 illustrates how we are to begin the marriage process. ***"That is why a man leaves his father and mother and is united to his wife, and they become one flesh." (Gen. 2:24 NIV).*** The key word in this verse is united. Used in the context of this verse, the Hebrew word for united (*dabaq*) means *hold fast, cling to, cause to cleave, press hard upon, be stuck together, to have close association, or tightly joined*. In other words, the two become one in every way. Another key concept to keep in mind in this passage is the concept of the wife being a suitable helper or helpmate for the husband. Wives are to help their husbands serve the Lord, as Eve was to help Adam take care of the Garden of Eden. Whether it be ministry, finances, child-rearing, household responsibilities or other areas of life that require work, the wife is to be a helpmate to the husband. If this basic principle is applied throughout marriage, the couple will have a successful life. This is how God intended for married couples to function. God did not intend for one person to do everything. The husband has the primary responsibility of being the head of the household and the wife is to be a helper suitable for him *(Gen. 2:18)*. Keep in mind that society does not teach this principle, however God does. So, it would be in your best interest as a couple to apply this principle to your marriage.

The Bible also gives us instructions on how we are to treat each other as husband and wife. On a day to day basis, we are to remind ourselves of how we are to relate to one another as a married couple. There is a certain way God wants us to interact with one another. One thing to keep in mind is that God did not intend for us to feel hindered or uncomfortable because of the way we treat our spouses. God wants us to live in a manner in which we feel loved, respected, and cherished by the one we are married to. Wives are to submit their husbands, as unto the Lord, and husbands are to be the head of the wives and they are to love their wives just as Christ loved the Church *(Ephesians 5:22-27)*. The love described here is sacrificial in nature. When men understand how much Christ loves the church and how he sacrificed His life for the body, we get a deeper understanding of how we are to love our wives. Wives should not be fearful of submitting to a husband who has submitted himself to the Lord. A man who loves the Lord should not dominate or mistreat his wife. Therefore, women should not avoid the submission clause in the scripture based on how the world views submission. Women should view submission to their husbands as their responsibility to God *(Colossians 3:17-18)*.

A couple must also keep in mind that marriage is a lifelong commitment. It is not something you can casually get out of if things don't go right or if one of the partners does not have his or her way. Somehow, mankind came up with the concept of divorce. Sadly, close to 50% of marriages in America end in divorce. The failure rate for second marriages is even higher. Divorce is a sin in God's eyes. Sin never solves any problems. Sin only leads to more problems and more pain. Divorce can be very painful emotionally and devastating financially. Worse than that, a couple that decides to divorce will suffer spiritually. The Bible clearly speaks out against divorce. In fact, God hates divorce *(Malachi 2:16)*. Jesus was questioned about divorce and he basically stated that divorce is forbidden unless there has been marital unfaithfulness (especially unrepentant adultery) on the part of one of the marriage partners *(Matthew 19:1-8)*. Jesus also forbids letting man end the marriage of another *(Matthew 19:6)*. In other words, Jesus does not want marriages to end in divorce based on the decision of a judge in a court of law!

The idea of separation may also come into play when difficulties in marriage arise. However, God does not approve of separation *(I Corinthians 7:10)*. If circumstances become so bad that separation is needed (ex. Physical abuse or mental cruelty), the couple is still required by God to eventually reconcile their differences after a time of separation *(I Corinthians 7:11)*. Prayerfully, your marriage will not have these kinds of issues. If as a couple you have decided to let God lead and guide you in marriage through the Word of God, you will be much better off. Love must be a major component of your marriage and the Bible gives a description of how real love looks and functions in the lives of believers *(I Corinthians 13: 4-10)*. One question we should ask ourselves is whether our love for one another fits the description of love described in the Corinthians passage.

One of the richest passages of scripture dealing with marriage is found in chapter 3 of I Peter. I would advise reading chapter 2 of this same book before digging into the information on marriage found in chapter 3. Wives are given clear instructions on how to be sincere, loving, and God-fearing women in their marriages *(I Peter 3:1-6)*. Inner beauty is a quality that wives should be concerned with as opposed to outer beauty. The world teaches women to focus on how they look, but God wants women to focus on having their beauty come from the inside. A beautiful woman can have a tremendous effect on a man. I am not speaking in the sense of outer beauty; I am speaking of how godly character in a woman can motivate a man to be what God intends for him to be. Husbands are encouraged to treat their wives in a loving manner that involves being considerate and respectful *(1 Peter 3:7)*. In fact, if a man wants to ensure that his prayers are heard, he must treat his wife the way God expects him to despite how she may behave or live. An important thought to keep in mind is that negative behavior on the part of one spouse does not justify negative behavior from the other spouse as a form of retaliation. Vengeance belongs to God, not us. Forgiveness is a spiritual discipline that will have to be practiced throughout the entire marriage. In fact, you will have to forgive each other to ensure that God forgives you of your sins *(Matthew 5:14-15)*. As married couples, we also must be careful not to judge one another *(Matthew 7:1-5)* when dealing with our faults, weaknesses, and sins.

As you can clearly see, the Bible is going to be needed as an instruction manual for the two of you for the marriage to flourish. God created marriage and God intends for marriage to function a certain way. To know what marriage truly is and what God's will for your marriage is, you must consult the Bible. If marriage were considered an academic course of study, the Bible would be the main textbook needed to pass the course. Do not put it down and do not disregard it throughout your marriage.

Your assignment for this session is listed below. Please read through the passages of scripture and discuss the parts that resonate with you. Discuss how you can apply what you have read to your future marriage.

Session One Homework

- Get a New International Version of the Bible
- Pray that God will speak to both of you through His word
- Read the book of Hosea
- Read chapter 2 of Genesis, paying close attention to verses 18 & 24
- Read Matthew 19:1-12
- Read Ephesians 5:21-32
- Read Colossians 3:17-19
- Read chapter 7 of I Corinthians and chapter I Corinthians 13:4-10
- Read I Peter 3:1-7
- Meditate on James 1:22-2

SESSION TWO

Temperament & Personality

Purpose: To help the couple understand how temperament and personality is critical in understanding who they are as individuals and how they will (or will not) relate to one another as a couple

Hopefully, each of you has a clear understanding of who you are and how your personality functions on a day-to-day basis. We must keep in mind that in many cases, the two of you may have only known each other for a few years. That short time span may or may not be sufficient for the two of you to know and understand each other. It is especially important that the two of you know who you are and how God designed you to be as individuals. By understanding who you really are, you can gain a better understanding of how to relate to one another. This will come into play as you learn how to **communicate** with each other properly. No one wants to be unhappy and not getting along with each other is one of the easiest ways to guarantee unhappiness.

In this session, we are going to look at a personality study that deals with temperaments in efforts to establish strengths and weaknesses in personality. By taking an honest look at who we are and how we function, we can hopefully ward off some potential personality clashes in the future.

The heart of the **temperament** theory as first conceived by Hippocrates over twenty-four hundred years ago divides people into four basic categories: sanguine, choleric, melancholy, and phlegmatic (LaHaye p. 25). Understanding these four temperaments can help a person discover their strengths and weaknesses. It can also help a person decide which career path they are best suited for. Most importantly, it can help a person improve some of their personality traits that may be hindering them in life and in their relationships with other people. Most people have one or more of these temperament types. Commonly, a person is usually a blend of two types with one being more dominant than the other. By figuring out what type of temperament blend you have, you can determine how to relate to someone who has a similar or different blend of temperament than your own. Let's look briefly at each type to get an idea of what they are like.

1. **Sanguine** -- This person is usually very lively and enjoyable. This person is an
outgoing extrovert type. This person usually has a lot of friends and they are often very talkative people. This person can be noisy and friendly at the same time. This person also has a
tendency to appear to be more confident on the outside than they really are on the inside. They also tend to be wrong when it comes to a lot of different issues.

2. **Choleric** -- This person is very practical and strong-willed. This person is usually self-sufficient, independent, decisive, and opinionated. He or she is usually not very sympathetic with others. This person is also goal oriented, dominant, bossy, and somewhat of an opportunist.

3. **Melancholy** -- This person is usually a very analytical, gifted, self-sacrificing perfectionist. This person gets enjoyment from the fine arts. However, this person is also very moody. This person is a faithful friend; however, negative experiences with people can put this person on guard. This person tends to choose a career path that will involve sacrifice and suffering to be successful. Unfortunately, depression is a common trait found in this person.

4. **Phlegmatic** -- This person is the calm, easygoing type that usually never gets upset.

This person is the most likeable and he or she is typically easy to get along with. Calm and cool are two words that describe this person. This person tends to be a spectator in life and he or she usually does not get involved in activities. This person seldom conveys their true feelings.

Most people are usually a blend of two of these temperament types. The chart on the next page shows common strengths and weaknesses of these four temperament types.

Temperament	Strengths	Weaknesses
Sanguine	Outgoing, Responsive, Warm & Friendly, Talkative, Enthusiastic, Compassionate	Undisciplined, Emotionally Unstable, Unproductive, Egocentric, Exaggerates
Choleric	Strong-willed, Independent, Visionary, Practical, Productive, Decisive, Leader	Cold & Unemotional, Self-sufficient, Impetuous, Domineering, Unforgiving, Sarcastic, Angry, Cruel
Melancholy	Gifted, Analytical, Aesthetic, Self-Sacrificing, Industrious, Self-Disciplined	Moody, Self-centered, Persecution-prone, Revengeful, Touchy, Theoretical, Unsociable, Critical, Negative
Phlegmatic	Calm, Quiet, Easygoing, Dependable, Objective, Diplomatic, Efficient, Organized, Practical	Unmotivated, Procrastinator, Selfish, Stingy, Self-Protective, Indecisive, Fearful, Worrier

Take some time to figure out which temperament each of you has. Be honest with yourselves. Do not say that you are someone that you really are not. Figure out if your personality is a blend of two types. The book, ***Why You Act the Way You Do?*** by Tim LaHaye is a great resource that will further aid in discovering your temperament. I encourage you to read this book together and discuss your findings. The purpose of this exercise is to help you better understand yourselves so you can relate to one another in your marriage. Understanding who you are will help you resolve conflict in an organized and effective manner. For example, knowing that you are a *sanguine* type married to a *choleric* type will help you choose the rights steps in relating to one another. Understanding who you are will help you improve your strengths and eliminate your weaknesses for you to be a better marriage partner. Please be prayerful about this session and make sure you are well prepared by reading and discussing the suggested material.

I would also like to encourage you to read Galatians 5:22-23 which describes the Fruit of the Spirit. Your behavior and personality traits should be guided by scriptural principles. This passage gives a great framework for a positive and strong temperament type with regards to overall behavior. Astrology or zodiac signs should not be the guidelines used with regards to behavior. I acknowledge that traits may be similar when analyzing people who are of a certain zodiac sign. But those behavioral aspects are not biblical or scriptural and they should not dictate our behavior. As you review Galatians 5:22-23, I would encourage you to keep these biblical principles in mind as you interact with one another.

When interacting with one another as a couple, we must practice behavioral traits such as love, joy, peace, forbearance (patience), kindness, gentleness, faithfulness, and self-control. If we do so, we can avoid arguments and disagreements with one another. In contrast, Galatians 5:19-21 lists all the character traits we want to avoid in dealing with one another and other people. If you look at the traits listed in this passage, a lot of them are comparable to the temperament weaknesses listed in the charts we just looked at. Thankfully, the character traits listed in Galatians 5:22-23 are very comparable to the temperament strengths that are listed in the chart we reviewed earlier. Again, this section in Apostle Paul's letter to the Galatians is a template for how believers should act towards one another. The acts of flesh, as Paul describes them, are obvious traits that we want to avoid. It would serve us well to follow Paul's advice.

Love is patient, love is kind. It does not envy, it does not boast, it is not proud. It does not dishonor others, it is not self-seeking, it is not easily angered, it keeps no record of wrongs. Love does not delight in evil but rejoices with the truth. It always protects, always trusts, always hopes, always perseveres. 1 Corinthians 13:4-8 NIV

Going a step further, I would encourage you to look at 1st Corinthians 13:4-8 in the Bible. This is what I like to call the love chapter. It gives a biblical framework with regards to loving God honoring behavior towards one another. For example, the *a* section of verse 4 of this passage starts off by stating that love is patient and kind. We have to learn how to practice patience and kindness towards one another. This verse ends with a contrast of what love is not as love does not boast nor is love proud. If we refer to our chart, we can easily see how being loving and kind is a strength in temperament, especially in a person with a Sanguine personality type. As you move to verse 5, you get more examples of what love is not. It does not dishonor others, it is not selfish or self-seeking, it is not easily angered, and it keeps no record of wrongs. A very weak, melancholy personality type exhibits these kinds of negative behavior. And this type of person is hard to get along with and hard to live with. It is better to know these things going into the marriage as opposed to finding out after you are married. If either of you exhibit this type of behavior, it is best to acknowledge it and pray that the Spirit of God will help you overcome these weaknesses in your personality.

As you read this passage of scripture further, it forces you to look in the mirror at yourself. Sadly, we often focus on what's wrong with our partner as opposed to what is wrong with us. Verse 6 starts off with a negative trait compared to a positive trait. Paul uses this language style to help us understand what we should be doing versus what we should not be doing as it pertains to our relationships with one another. As we look at our personality types and the weaknesses that come with them, we can determine what types of behavior we want to avoid. Verse 7 is extremely positive. The strengths of the Phlegmatic personality type are displayed in the positive love qualities that Paul encourages us to utilize. The first sentence in verse 8 encourages us by stating that, "Love never fails." A strong person with any of the four personality types will succeed in living in harmony in their marriages. These aspects of love never fail in dealing with one another. As you discover why you act the way you do, be encouraged in knowing that the Bible can help you overcome your weakness. These two passages we just looked at represent a good starting point. Fortunately, there are other passages of scripture that can help us in our dealings with one another to have harmony in our marriages.

Session Two Homework

1. Determine your temperament type
2. Discuss ways that your temperament types may complement or conflict with one another
3. Read and discuss the book *Why You Act the Way You Do* by Tim LaHaye
4. Read Galatians 5:19-21 and 5:22-23
5. Read 1 Corinthians 13:4-8

SESSION THREE

Sexuality

Purpose: To understand how the sexual relationship is supposed to function in the marriage and how important it is to the health of the marriage

The two of you may be wondering why we are going to discuss this topic. You may even be embarrassed with the fact that I have brought it up. However, you must understand that the sexual relationship you will have in your marriage is very important. Sexual compatibility is essential in your relationship. Your sexual relationship is going to mirror the function or dysfunction of your marriage relationship. What I mean by this is that problems in your marriage will come out in your sex life. If your relationship is the way God intended it to be and it is functioning properly based on biblical principles, your sex life will more than likely reflect this fact in a fulfilling manner for both of you.

We must also keep in mind that just as God created marriage for a purpose, God also created our sexuality for a purpose. However, just as mankind has abused and misused the institution of marriage, mankind also has abused sexuality. This abuse has taken place throughout history dating all the back to the Sodom & Gomorrah incident in the Bible. Homosexuality (sex between two people of the same gender) has always been a problem. Rape is nothing new. One of David's sons raped his sister, for example. Today we see problems such as homosexuality, rape, pornography, masturbation, teen pregnancies, abortions, incest, pedophilia, and sexual harassment in the workplace all as part of a long list of sexual misconduct that is destroying our society. It seems as if Satan is exploiting Christians and non-Christians through the abuse of sexuality and sexual relations. God never intended for sex to be this way. Sex was designed for married people only! The sexual relationship between a man and a woman in the context of a marriage only was created by God for a purpose. The birth of children was meant to take place in the context of a marriage through a healthy, sexual relationship between husband and wife.

If you have not engaged in sexual relations with each other, that is wonderful, and you are to be commended. I would ask that you continue to abstain until you get married. If you have engaged in sexual relations, I ask that you first confess this sin to God and ask him to forgive you for indulging in fornication. I also ask that you repent of this sin and abstain from engaging in sexual activity from this day forward until you are married. God will forgive if you confess this sin (1 John 1:9). Understand that if you chose to ignore my request, you leave yourselves open to suffer the consequences of your sinful behavior in one way or another.

If either of you is sexually active outside of your committed relationship, I encourage you to cease your activity. Confess your fornication to God, ask for his forgiveness, and repent of this sinful behavior. You do not want to develop soul ties and relationships that you will have to sever immediately when you get married. Nor do you want to develop sexual appetites that your spouse may be unable or unwilling to satisfy. You definitely do not want to compare your spouse to former lovers or hold them to standards that another lover may have set regarding your sexual fulfillment. You don't want to go into your marriage with the possibility of committing adultery because you are involved in a sexual relationship that you are having trouble cutting off.

If the two of you are living together, I would ask that you make living arrangements to reside separately from now until the day of the wedding. By being in the same house and possibly sleeping in the same bed, you will be tempting yourselves to indulge in sexual activity. This may cause you an inconvenience, however it is best that you not live together prior to marriage. You also both need to be tested physically for things such as H.I.V. You want to enter your marriage with a clean bill of physical and sexual health. It is also probably best that the two of

THE MIRACLE OF ONENESS

you do not discuss your past sexual history unless there are some major health issues or concerns involved.

Finally, let's look briefly at what the Bible says about sexuality in relation to marriage. Genesis 2:24 is the scripture we commonly think of pertaining to marriage. The last part of this verse is key to the sexual relationship. They will become one flesh *(Genesis 2:24)*. The becoming of one flesh symbolizes the oneness of the marital relationship in several ways. It symbolizes oneness emotionally, spiritually, socially, and in the case of sexuality, physical oneness. Childbirth is to come as a result of the sexual relationship between husband and wife *(Genesis 4:1)*. The sexual relationship is to be kept pure and within the confines of the marriage *(Hebrews 13:4)*. Sex outside of marriage is forbidden *(Exodus 20:14)*. Unrepentant adultery is the only biblical reason for divorce (Matthew 19:9). However, marital unfaithfulness can involve things other than sex. The key is that the guilty party confesses and is forgiven by the other person. In cases of adultery (or marital unfaithfulness), God would prefer that the two of you reconcile and exercise forgiveness. There is even an incident in the Bible that involves a husband reconciling with his unfaithful wife *(Hosea 3:1)*. However, the choice to forgive and move past an affair on the part of one of the partners will require great strength and spiritual maturity) on the part of the person who has been cheated on.

Not meeting the sexual needs of your spouse can lead to problems such as adultery. In fact, neglecting one another sexually is forbidden *(I Corinthians 7:5)*. Health issues may cause married couples to abstain but purposely abstaining is only allowed if that time is going to be devoted to prayer and fasting *(I Corinthians 7:5)*. Sex should never be used as a form of control, reward, or punishment. Read the "Song of Solomon" in the Bible to get a good picture of how a healthy sexual relationship is supposed to look in a marriage.

Be prepared to openly discuss with your partner all the issues I mentioned that pertain to sexuality. Please try to abstain from this day forward leading up to your wedding day. Read the scriptures listed in this written session and discuss them. Meditate on them separately and be prepared to share how these scriptures can be applied in your marriage. The sexual relationship is meant to be a celebration of the marriage. It is particularly important that you enter marriage with a healthy, biblical perspective on the topic of sexuality. During your marriage, communicate with each other about this issue. If problems arise in the sex life of your marriage, seek counseling immediately. As I stated earlier, the sexual dysfunction of your marriage will probably be the result of a bigger issue or problem that needs to be dealt with.

Make it your goal to have a sexual relationship that is not only fulfilling to both of you, but at the same time glorifying to God. You are supposed to enjoy your sexual relationship (*Proverbs 5:18-19*). Be creative. Read Christian books about sexuality. Remember that you have a lifetime to develop a great sexual relationship. Do your best to make sure that the night of your honeymoon is special. Abstaining from this day forward will make it even more special for the two of you. Prayerfully consider all the suggestions and requests I have made. You will benefit from them as a couple. Thank you.

Session Three Homework

- Abstain from engaging in pre-marital sex
- Devote yourself to a time of celibacy prior to getting married
- Adjust living arrangements if you currently stay together
- Read, meditate, and discuss these passages of scriptures together: Genesis 2:24, Genesis 4:1, Hebrews 3:4, Exodus 20:14, 1 Corinthians 7:5, Proverbs 5:18-19
- Read the book Song of Solomon to understand healthy sexual relationships

SESSION FOUR

The Goal of Marriage

Purpose: To clearly define the goal of marriage and to determine what goals the couple will strive to meet in their marriage

One question that I would like to ask you at this time is why have you decided to get married? Surprisingly, many couples jump into marriage not knowing why they are getting married. Worse than that, a lot of couples have no understanding of what the purpose or goal of marriage is. To make matters even worse, most couples do not have a defined goal or purpose in mind when they decide to get married.

What is the real goal of marriage? Most of us think the goal of marriage deals with things such as sex, companionship, love, children, social acceptance, economic advantage, and security (Chapman, p. 57). Honestly, most people in society already have things such as sex, companionship, love, and children without getting married. For example, there are many single women who want to have kids so desperately that they turn to measures such as artificial insemination to have children. There are plenty of men who donate sperm or who simply get women pregnant the natural way without the thought of marriage or even an intimate relationship. In fact, many people don't give it much thought at all. Some people marry just to have a family, or they marry because they had children out of wedlock. For some, marriage is convenient financially because one of the partners makes enough money to take care of both of them and a family.

Some marry because at a certain age (especially the age of 30) it is the socially acceptable thing to do. Sadly, because of these different motives, many people are getting married for the wrong reasons. Their negative motives end up in a marriage filled with issues that ultimately become a disaster. One of the partners may not live up to their part of the bargain. The finances may not be like they imagined. The romance or the sexual relationship may change or die down in passion after a few years, childbirth, and weight gain by both partners. When we do things in life with no purpose or goal in mind, those things usually end up in failure.

A decision as important as marriage must be one made with a clear goal in mind. Once again, we need to ponder the question, 'What is the goal of marriage?' I believe that **the goal of marriage is for a man and woman to unite as one in a relationship that honors God and reflects the love relationship between God and His children.** The statement I just made is an example of a mission statement that can be used to define the purpose or goal of marriage. In the question section of this session, I ask that the two of you write out a clear mission statement that will define the goal and purpose of your marriage. I believe that it is also important to ask yourself, "Why do I believe the present time is right for us to get married?" Before answering this question, I want both of you to pray about this together. Timing is especially important. There are a lot of different things to consider with regards to timing. For example, the date that you choose to get married will always be your anniversary date. You want that date to have a significant meaning to the two of you. The season of the year may or may not be important to you. Some people prefer to marry during the summer months especially if they want a part or all of the wedding to be outdoors. I have officiated at least four wedding ceremonies outdoors. I have had mixed experiences. For example, it rained, and it was very windy outside on one occasion in which the wedding took place in early October. Another time in early August, it was 95 degrees outside with no wind at all. On two other occasions, the wedding ceremony was held at Buckingham Fountain in Chicago and the aesthetics were beautiful. The weather was great, and the pictures were wonderful. Timing is everything when it comes to choosing a wedding date. Timing affects a lot of other factors as well.

For example, is this the right time for both of you financially? Can you afford the wedding ceremony that you desire? I will discuss this question further in the next session on finances. But let's consider a couple of questions now. Is spending money on an elaborate wedding going to cause you to start off your marriage in a financial hole? Are you simply going to go into the Pastor's office or to the courthouse to exchange vows? And now that I am bringing up a church related issue, this leads to my next question about the goals of your marriage.

Church attendance and church membership are both especially important, and this subject is definitely one to consider when you are looking at the goal or purpose of your marriage. You may be wondering why I'm bringing up this subject now. It's because this is crucial to the development and viability of your marriage. Notice in the mission statement I shared earlier that a big part of the goal of marriage is whether your marriage reflects the love relationship between God and His children. I pray that both of you have given your lives to Christ! This is critical if you are going to get married. Jesus Christ has to be the center of your marital relationship. In order for that to happen, you have to be a believer of our Lord and Savior, Jesus Christ. If one or both of you are not saved, I think we have to pause right now and consider the words of **Romans 10:9.** *"If you declare with your mouth, "Jesus is Lord, and believe in your heart, God raised Him from the dead, you will be saved."* It is key that both of you are saved. This is key as you trying to determine the goal of your marriage. The two of you have to be on the same page. If only one knows the Lord and the other one doesn't, I caution you strongly to reconsider entering into your marriage unequally yoked. Your goal in marriage should not be to change each other after you get married. Sadly, there are some people who believe that they can change their unbelieving partner into a believer once they get married. Both parties should already be believers! In other words, you should be equally yoked prior to getting married.

There has to be some level of spiritual maturity on the part of both of you prior to getting married. You cannot foolishly hope that one of you will just miraculously grow up spiritually after the wedding. It could happen! But there is also the possibility that it will not happen. Yes, there are couples where one spouse is led to Christ through the marriage. But let's be honest, this is a rare exception, and this is why you must pay careful attention to the timing of when you are going to get married. The timing from a spiritual standpoint affects the goal of the marriage. There has to be a unified path toward spiritual maturity in the midst of your goal as a married couple that honors God.

So, if you are both saved and true believers, at some point you will have to decide what church you will attend. You may already attend the same church and that is a beautiful thing. My wife and I initially met at the church we were attending at the time. But there was a period of time while we were dating in which we attended different churches. In fact, for the first two and a half years of our marriage, we regularly visited each other's church. Finally, in 2017, I joined the church my wife was attending. We had detailed conversations about this prior to marriage and it worked out the way God intended. The fact that we are both believers kept us from having any real issues about church. However, you can see how this issue can cause conflict as you try to create a mission statement for your marriage. How involved you will be in church can have a positive or negative impact on your marriage. How active will you serve in ministry? For example, will one of you sing on the praise team or in the choir or is one of you a minister or a leader in the church you attend? Or will you simply be lay members or parishioners? That is perfectly fine as well. Communication will be a crucial part in openly discussing these aspects of your marriage. As you prepare to discover the goal and purpose of your marriage, it should be clear to both of you that God has to be at the center of the foundation of your union. This will make it much easier for you to determine the goal of your marriage.

After you leave church each Sunday, you will have to return to your home that you share with your spouse. As you consider the goal of your marriage, you must deal with the issue of where you will live. If you are young, are you simply getting married so that you can move out of your parents' house? Is this the right time to do that? Or if you are an older or more seasoned couple, will you be purchasing a new home after the wedding? This is an important aspect of your marriage that fits into the big picture of your overall marriage goal. The size of the home you will live in is key because you may want to start a family, or you may be getting ready to blend your families into one unified household. Will you have children after you get married and if so, how many? If you want children, how soon do you want to start working on having them? This has to be considered and discussed prior to marriage especially when you are trying to determine the goal of your marriage. Again, you want your marriage to honor God and reflect the love relationship between God and His children. This comes into play when you are dealing with each other and the other members of your family, large or small. As we will see later in this guide, children or multiple family members can be costly from a financial standpoint. There must be some financial goals in place as you strive to construct the goal or the big picture of your marriage.

How will you handle your finances? In the next chapter, we will take a more detailed look at many financial issues that need to be considered. If your goal of marriage is clear and succinct, you will have a much easier time setting financial goals. What financial career goals do each of you have as individuals? How can you consolidate your individual financial goals for the benefit of your marriage? A healthy marriage is financially healthy. However, a healthy marriage is also healthy from a physical standpoint.

Do either of you have any special health issues or concerns? If so, how will you manage these issues? Are the two of you communicating about your doctors' visits and the regularity of those visits? Again, you want your marriage to honor God and we honor God by taking care of our physical temples. You should know the name of the doctor of your future husband or wife. You should know what medications either of you are taking and why you are taking it. This sounds personal and intrusive, but there must be transparency regarding these topics going into the marriage. It would be very hurtful if one of both of you became ill without disclosing your physical health issues prior to the wedding day. This is one reason why a clean bill of health should be given before you enter into the marriage. This marriage is for a lifetime and I pray that both of you will live to grow old together. Let's honor God by being honest with one another regarding our health status. It may seem like you are crossing boundaries by getting personal with the physical history of the person you are about to marry. However, the reality is that boundaries must be established or maintained properly for your marriage to be successful and God honoring.

Speaking of physical boundaries, let's discuss boundaries in general. Will you set boundaries in various areas of life to help protect your relationship? Are you both very private in areas of your life and do you get offended if you feel you partner is crossing a boundary? There cannot be invisible boundaries. You have to talk openly about your likes, dislikes, and expectations in order for your marriage to thrive. If your goal is truly honoring God and reflecting His love in your relationship, you must agree on several clear boundaries before marriage. It will serve both of you well by doing so. This will help you get to know each other better as you strive to clearly define the goal of your marriage.

Let's talk about how well the two of you know each other. This will make goal setting much easier for both of you. Do you honestly feel like you know each other well enough to get married? There is no set timeframe on how long it takes to truly get to know one another. You are going to spend the rest of your lives getting to know each other, but there should be a level of comfort present with regards to how well you know each other. Your values should be similar. This will depend on how you were raised by one or both of your parents. You may or may not have had a marriage model in view all your life. My parents were married for 52 years before my father passed. I grew up observing their marriage and a lot of my beliefs and values surrounding marriage came from what I observed in their marriage. Their marriage was based on biblical principles. It was not a perfect marriage, but it honored God. Are you prepared to have a marriage built on biblical principles? I would strongly encourage you to build your marriage on a biblical and spiritual foundation.

The reality that is that both of you may have some doubts and fears as you enter the marriage covenant. We don't live in a perfect world. We are all sinners and we all have fallen short of God's standards (Romans 3:23). So, let's address your fears and concerns head on now so that that they won't become an issue in your future marriage. Do you have any doubts or fears concerning certain issues that may hinder you in marriage? If the answer is yes, I would encourage you to discuss these issues openly and honestly.

Another aspect to consider is how your parents feel about your upcoming marriage. Are your parents supportive of your marriage? If not, why? If they are supportive of your marriage, it will make things a lot easier for you. I would implore you to learn from their example of marriage. Look at the good and the bad. Look at the victories and the mistakes. You can learn a lot from simply observing your parents or other more seasoned married couples that you may admire.

I was fortunate and blessed to have a marriage model of my parents that I observed all my life. However, one or both of you may have witnessed other couples going through a divorce. You may have even gone through a divorce yourself. I am transparent enough to admit that this is my second marriage, and it is my wife, Keyonna's second marriage as well. If you have gone through a divorce, I pray that you learned every lesson possible in lieu of that situation. The gracious and forgiving God we serve will give you another chance if you choose to honor Him in your marriage going forward. I can speak from experience that the lack of a clear goal in your marriage will ultimately lead to failure and I would not wish divorce on anyone. I pray that both of you will seek God together as you prepare for your marriage.

Let's be clear. Marriage is a covenant. Marriage is meant to last for the duration of your lifetime. Do you fully understand that marriage is a lifelong commitment, and that divorce is not an option? Do you passionately believe that God has placed the two of you together to be husband and wife? Marriage is a beautiful thing. It is especially beautiful when marriage honors God. To the men reading this guide, keep in mind that **"He who finds a wife finds what is good and receives favor from the Lord." (Proverbs 18:22)** Ladies, God can bless you with a Boaz the way He blessed Ruth. The marriage covenant is one of God's greatest gifts to His children. Are the two of you truly prepared to honor the marriage covenant? I pray that both of you will discover the supreme goal of the marriage covenant that you are about to enter.

In his best-selling book, *Growing Toward Marriage*, Gary Chapman defines the supreme purpose (or goal) of marriage as "the union of two individuals at the deepest possible level and in all areas, which in turn brings the greatest possible sense of fulfillment to the couple and at the same time serves the best purposes of God for their lives. (Chapman p. 59) Oneness between the couple in every area of life (spiritually, emotionally, financially, sexually) is the key factor. In fact, the principle of **oneness** in my definition and Chapman's definition is what God had in mind when he ordained the first marriage found in the Bible *(Genesis 2:24)*.

God intended for married couples to be **one** with each other. All the things I mentioned earlier as the normal goals of marriage do come into play throughout the union. In marriage, there is sex, love, companionship, children, security, and social acceptance. However, these things should not be the main or only reasons for getting married. For example, a man should not marry a woman just because he wants to have license to have sex with her for the rest of his life. Nor should a woman marry a man only because he will provide financial security for her. These things are all a part of the big picture. And the big picture is **oneness**.

For this session's homework, I want you to focus on and address a series of questions. Please answer these questions together openly and honestly. Discuss your answers with one another. Pray that God will show the two of you what His purpose is for you as a couple. Even though oneness should be your main concern, think about some practical issues that tie into the concepts of oneness as well as your daily lives. You will also craft a purpose statement unique to your relationship.

Session Four Homework

Honestly answer and discuss the following questions together:

- What is the goal of marriage in general?
- **What is the goal and/or purpose of your marriage?** (Create your purpose/mission statement.)
- Why do you believe the present time is right for you to get married?

- Where will you live once you get married?
- Will you be purchasing a home?
- Will you have children after you get married and if so, how many?
- If you want children, how soon do you want to start working on having them?
- How will you handle your finances?
- What career goals do each of you have as individuals?
- What church will you attend?
- How active will you be in ministry?
- Do either of you have any special health issues or concerns? If so, how will you
- manage these issues?
- Will you set boundaries in various areas of life to help protect your relationship?
- Do you honestly feel like you know each other well enough to get married?
- Are prepared to have a marriage built on biblical principles?
- Do you have any doubts or fears concerning certain issues that may hinder you in
   marriage?
- Are your parents supportive of your marriage? If not, why?
- Do you fully understand that marriage is a lifelong commitment and that divorce
   is not an option?
- Do you passionately believe that God has placed the two of you together to be husband and wife?
- Are you truly prepared to honor the marriage covenant?
- Finally, do you feel you need more preparation and guidance in any topic concerning marriage that we have or have not discussed?
- As an extra assignment, read the book of Ruth together. The marriage that develops at the end of that book is a beautiful example of a union coming together in a Godly manner.

Gregory L. Payton

SESSION FIVE

Finances

Purpose: To discuss the issue of finances and to come up with a plan for the handling of finances during the marriage

One of the biggest reasons for failure in marriage is the area of finances. Money issues tend to cause issues for many married couples. Because of this fact, I feel that it is crucial that financial issues be discussed prior to marriage to avoid conflict. We also need to look at ways of handling finances so that when you enter marriage, you have a financial plan in place that will help maintain peace and order in the home. We also need to look at whether either of you have current financial issues that you are dealing with. These issues need to be addressed and possibly corrected before entering a marriage.

The questions at the end of this chapter need to be addressed by the both of you. Brace yourself; the list is long! There may even be some things I left out. However, the issue of finances is extremely critical in marriage. Be sure to address each one of them. There are general finance questions and there are financial issues concerning the wedding ceremony that I would like to address at this time. I have listed a few questions for you to consider regarding the wedding ceremony. I think this will be of much benefit to you. Please pray together concerning all the questions asked. You have a month to look at all the issues. There may be many other questions and potential issues you can think of that relate to the area of finances. Be prepared for a very lengthy session together on this topic. In the end, I believe both of you will be glad that you addressed these issues prior to marriage.

A serious question to consider right now is "at this present moment, are both of you financially stable"? Openness and honesty regarding this question is particularly important. Financial issues can destroy a marriage quickly. If one (or both) of you has current financial issues, what are they?

And what caused the financial issues that you have? Did bad spending habits get you into a situation that you are having a hard time getting out of. If either of you have filed for bankruptcy recently or in the past, be honest about it. It would be devastating if this issue came out after you are married. For example, if you are in the process of making any type of purchase after you get married, it would be painful for either of you to find out for the first time that there was a bankruptcy in your past. You want may even consider reviewing each other's credit reports prior to marriage. Do either of you have major credit card debt? Do either of you have collections on your credit report? Credit checks are done whenever a major purchase is being made or when you are applying for loans or financing. The marriage that you are about enter is a major step that you are both about to make. So, conducting a credit check of both parties is not out of order in any way.

Which one of you is good at handling money? This question requires a lot of honesty and transparency. Think carefully before you answer it. If you are dishonest about this issue, the truth will come out through your spending habits and patterns on the future. Mishandling finances can have a devastating effect on your marriage. So, it is best to best honest with each other with regards to the handling of money and finances. It does not make either of you less of a person if one of you is better at handling money than the other. A decision on this issue is for the benefit of your marriage.

If both of you are good at it, who is going to be the primary handler? Pride has no place with regards to making this decision. One partner domineering the other has no place in marriage when it comes to handling finances. If both of you are bad at handling money, how will you educate yourselves to get better? Do not be afraid to seek help with regards to this issue. You do not want to face bankruptcies or foreclosures in your marriage. Peace and harmony will exist in your marriage if your finances are managed properly.

Let's look at some specific and typical purchases that couples make when they get married. Where you plan to live is a major area of concern and how you plan to finance this aspect of your marriage is something that you need to discuss openly and honestly. Are you going to purchase a house after the wedding? Or do you plan on renting until you are financially stable enough to buy a home? If both of you already own property, a decision must be made as to which location you plan to live in. If only one of you owns property at this time and the other person is going to move into the home of the spouse that is paying a mortgage already, there are several items that needs to be discussed upfront. For example, are you going to split the mortgage? Are you going to alternate paying the mortgage from season to season? My wife and I agreed that we would alternate payment of the mortgage based on the academic school year. My wife is an educator in the Chicago Public School system. I pay the mortgage during the summer months because my wife does not work during the summer months when school is out. This arrangement works perfectly for us. As a couple, you must take time and planning to figure out what works best for you. What works for one couple may not work for another couple. Finally, if you enter the marriage before you become homeowners, you must develop a savings plan and financing plan to help you work towards the goal of owning your own home.

The next item we will look is transportation. Owning a vehicle may seem like a small issue, but it is a serious financial matter. One or both of you may be currently financing or leasing a vehicle (Car, Truck, SUV, etc.). Or one or both of you may own a vehicle that is paid for. However, the cost of maintenance of a vehicle that is paid for can be challenging depending on what shape the vehicle is in. There are several things that must be discussed such as how many vehicles you will have for example? If there is only one vehicle, will you share that vehicle? If one or both of you decide that you want a new vehicle, are you willing to sacrifice and save for that new vehicle? Open and honest communication is needed with regards to this area of your marriage. Vehicle ownership and maintenance can be a nonexistent source of confusion or it can be a huge source of contention and confusion. It is imperative that both of you have realistic taste with regards to what you want to drive. In other words, your marriage cannot afford for either of you to live beyond your means. Purchasing a new vehicle is something that everyone will have to deal with as the years go buy. This is a big financial decision that must be well thought out and openly communicated between the two of you. As a man, you may want that fancy sports car or that pickup truck that you always wished for.

Ladies, you may want a luxury car or S.U.V. (Sports Utility Vehicle) or you may want a minivan that will hold more than one child. As I transition to the next item of discussion, we must consider whether a bigger vehicle is needed because of the number of children you may have to transport at one time. You want your children to be comfortable and safe especially if you must put in a cart seat for the babies that you may have in the future. So, let's talk about kids now that we have considered vehicles and the subject of transportation as a whole.

CHILDREN are a gift or heritage from the Lord according to the Bible in Psalm 127:3. How many children you plan to have is a serious question that you must ask each other on so many levels (spiritually, emotionally, and financially). Let's be real, raising children is expensive. There must be an honest discussion about whether you want to have children or not. Naturally, this decision could change during the marriage, but it is best to be honest about your intentions and your desires regarding the issue of having children. Depending on your circumstances or your history or your age, you may be coming into this marriage with children from a previous relationship or marriage. Blended families are a reality in the 21st century. The dynamics of your family will depend on the children that are already a part of the family or those that will become a part of the family in the future. I will use my marriage as an example of how children can set the tone for your household. I have a blended family and I am not ashamed to admit that reality. My wife and I both had 2 children each from our previous marriages. We had a child together a year into our marriage. So, we have a blended family with children that range greatly in age. In fact, my sons (Julian and Justin) from my prior marriage are both adults at this present time. They do not live with us, but they had a great impact on us financially at the beginning of our marriage. My wife's two children (Jayden & Jayla) are teenagers, and they live with us. Finally, the baby (Gabrielle) is 5 years old and I like to refer to her as the glue that connects all 5 of them together. But the reality is that Keyonna and I must financially provide for 3 children. This requires communication and sacrifice as well as strategic planning on how things function in our blended family. If neither of you have children prior to the marriage, you still must communicate and plan accordingly when it comes to children.

You may only want One child. You may not want any children. Or you may want multiple children. The reality that you must face as a couple is that it is expensive to raise children today. For example, will they attend private or public school? Are you going to start saving for their college education while they are young? This is going to require a lot of communication, discipline, and sacrifice. And yes, these things need to be discussed before your WEDDING.

And since I am talking about education and its financial implications, I cannot assume that one or both of you are college educated. If one or both of you have a college degree, praise God! But realistically, this issue leads to a series of financial questions that need to be discussed prior to the wedding day and your marriage in general. If either of you have a college degree, are there still outstanding loans that need to be paid off? I am blessed and fortunate that I had a lot of help financing the two degrees that I earned. My parents, my place of employment, the church I attended, and the scholarships that were awarded to me all helped to make my college education a reality. I had to finance a large portion of my master's degree myself. Overall, it was not cheap by any means. I do not have any college loan debt, but this is not everyone's reality. This subject must be discussed before you commit to marriage and a wedding. After your get married, are either of you considering graduate level education? And If so, how will you pay for it? Or are you both done with your educational pursuits? And even if you have finished school, I must again bring up the subject of outstanding student loan debt. It can hurt your marriage before you get started. Student loan debt can keep you from going on a honeymoon after the wedding. Student loan debt can make it harder for you to purchase a home if you plan to do so after a wedding. Student loan debt can cause you to need assistance financing your wedding. You may have to scale down depending on how extravagant you want your wedding to be. Student loan debt is a financial issue that we hate to talk about, but if it is a part of your reality, please discuss it before your wedding day. If these issues come up later in the marriage and it is the first time that one of you hears about it or learns about it, the effect could be devastating to your marriage.

This is a perfect transition in to the next topic I want to discuss with regards to finances and that is the subject of your work or employment careers. There must be honest disclosure about your employment and what you do for a living. Without an income or joint incomes, your marriage will not function or thrive financially. Are you both satisfied in your careers? In other words, do you like your jobs? This is important. This must be discussed openly and honestly before you try to plan a wedding and ultimately your marriage. Are you satisfied with the salary you make? Is your salary enough to support two adults. Or will your combined income allow the two of you to function and thrive as a couple? Are both of you going to work? If one of you is not going to work, why? And before either of you ask, there must be full disclosure about what you make annually. Do not be afraid to ask your future partner what his or her salary is. And do not feel intimidated if one of you makes more than the other. In the real world, you will have to consider if will have a joint checking account or separate accounts. In the question section at the end of this chapter, I have listed some specific questions that need to be asked and discussed before you can start planning your wedding and your life together as husband and wife.

Before I get to the wedding finances later in this chapter, I want to discuss church finances. As believers, we must always honor God with our finances. How will you honor God with your finances as a married couple? Or will you rob or jack God when it comes to the subject of money? Consider the words of Malachi 3 verse 8. " Will a mere mortal rob God? Yet You rob me. "But you ask, how are we robbing you? "In tithes and offerings". So, ask each other this question: Are you a tither? Are both of you in agreement with this biblical principle? Is it a strain or a burden for you to give offerings at the church you attend? If not, there are going to be some problems in your marriage (Malachi 3:9). And if God is truly at the center of your marriage relationship, tithing and giving to the church should not be an issue for either of you. In case you are reading this book and you do not understand the biblical practice of tithing, it is defined as giving ten percent of your income before taxes to the local church or ministry that you are a part of (Malachi 3:10a). This principle is not negotiable. It is for your benefit (Malachi 3:10b). So as believers, the two of you must discuss how much of your monthly income will be given to the church in tithes and offerings. Finally, a tithe is what you owe, and an offering is what you sow!

The next subject I want to discuss is something that you probably are not fond of. We cannot talk about income or finances without mentioning the IRS. And yes, this conversation must take place before the wedding. How will you file your income taxes? Will you file jointly or separately? If you get a refund, what will you do with it? Do you owe back taxes? Is the IRS looking for you or are you on their call list? Do either of you have a gambling problem? Do either of you habitually play the lottery? If so, are you willing to stop immediately? Do either of you have a problem with compulsive or impulsive spending? Do either of you have a problem or obsession with shopping? Is amazon your best friend? Is your amazon cart full right now? Are you a chronic downloader of music or movies like I am? And if you love to eat like I do, how will you buy groceries? Which of you will be responsible for this task or will you share it? Who is going to be responsible for paying the bills? Are you going to split the utilities or will one of you pay the utilities? I mentioned the mortgage earlier. What about car payments and car insurance? With all these expenses, how will you realistically budget the money you earn? How much will you spend on entertainment monthly or weekly? One or both of you may love to go to live concerts or movies or live plays.

These things cost money. While you are dating, you can kind of get a sense of what you like or dislike. One or both of you may like to go out to eat at nice restaurants. That is all fine and good while you are dating, but what happens once you are married; and you have responsibilities such as the ones we have discussed throughout this chapter.

Weddings are expensive and they require saving money. This will affect your dating habits and your entertainment preferences. If you plan on giving each other rings, you will have to scale back on your spending habits to get rings that you will both be satisfied with. Traditionally , there are couples who will not start planning a wedding until an engagement ring is put on the woman's finger. So, let us consider the question of whether or not you plan on saving a certain amount of money during a specific period for a specific purpose? This is going to have be done if you want a nice wedding. This is going to have to be done if you plan to purchase a home before or after the wedding. Sadly, we don't always think about these things before we walk down the aisle to say "I do". And therefore, so many marriages fail. There must be planning as well as open and honest communication. I would suggest that the two of you meet with a financial counselor or planner before getting married. This is not my area of expertise. I can only give you practical or biblical counsel in this area. But it would be wise and beneficial for the two of you to have a conversation or meeting with a skilled financial counselor or advisor. You can discuss this such as whether you are going to invest your money in stocks or CDs. You can talk through things such as the fact the one or both of you plan on participating in a 401K plan at your place of employment. And yes, you should briefly discuss some retirement plans or goals prior to marriage. You may be young, but time flies and before you know it, it will be time to start considering retirement. To retire comfortably, you must plan ahead and early. Your charitable giving or the lack thereof should be discussed as well. Do you plan on donating to any charities? Finally, you must look at where you are now financially and where you hope to in the future as a couple. Where do the two of you see yourself financially in 5 years? 10 years? 20 years?

    Wedding ceremonies can be awfully expensive. As you prepare for marriage, you must remember that you cannot start off your marriage journey by putting yourself in a financial hole because of spending money on a wedding that neither of you can afford. Some couples choose to have small ceremonies and that is perfectly fine. Some couples simply chose to have the officiant and a small number of witnesses present as they exchange vows. There is nothing wrong with that. We must get rid of the mindset of trying impress others with an extravagant wedding that is not feasible financially. Our EGO's cause us to focus on things that can damage your marriage before it starts. The word EGO can be used an acronym known as "Edging God Out". If God is the center of your marriage, the type of wedding you have will reflect your values as a believer. Ladies, you may have always had dreams of an extravagant wedding and it is perfectly fine to have those type of dreams. But at some point, reality sets in and you have to do what is best for both of you. If the two of you plan, strategize, and save money accordingly, you can have that dream wedding. My advice to you is to take your time. Do not rush into something that neither of you can afford. Dreams can become reality through prayer and transparency regarding where you are financially as a couple. All things are possible with God. Quoting the words of Jesus Christ: "what is impossible with man is possible with God." (Luke 18:27 NIV)

In closing I ask this question: Are you prepared to be forgiving and patient with one another if financial issues arise? Luke 6:37 encourages us to forgive one another so that we will be forgiven. Financial issues will put you in a place where you will have to forgive one another for mistakes that may be made. Financial issues will test your patience. This area of marriage requires the giving of grace to the spouse who may have financial issues. Will you help one another if either of you run into problems such as a layoff from a job? Will you stand by each other in tough financial times? Your marriage vows indicate that you will stay together for better or worse. Finances and money issues sadly fall into the worse category at times. We must go into marriage knowing that the possibility of these things happening is a reality. We cannot live in a financial fantasy world. Will you support and encourage each other concerning finances (and possible financial issues)? Will you loan each other money, or will you treat the money you both earn as belonging to both of you? If you know that you have a bad habit of not paying people back when you borrow money from them, the worst thing you can do is bring this bad habit into your marriage. Consider this verse when it comes to the issue of borrowing. "The wicked borrow and do not repay" (Psalm 37: 21A NIV). It is sinful and wicked to borrow money and not pay it back. This applies to taking out and loans and missing payments as well. If one of you makes more than the other, will this be an issue (especially if the female earns more)? Will there be resentment or competitiveness because one spouse makes more money than the other? I pray that both of you are mature enough to not let this be an issue. Both of you know how you feel about this type of issue. Be honest with yourselves. And if you are both mature enough to not make an issue of who earns more, Praise God! Ask yourselves honestly if you are prepared to work together as a team when it comes to finances. The Bible gives us encouragement with regards to working together as a couple financially.

"Two are better than one, because they have a good return for their labor: If either of them falls down, one can help the other up. But pity anyone who falls and has no one to help them up."
(Ecclesiastes 4:9-10 NIV)

Session Five Homework

Honestly answer the following questions together:

General Finance Questions

- At this present moment, are both of you financially stable?
- If one (or both) of you has current financial issues, what are they?
- Which one of you is good at handling money? If both of you are good at it, who is going to be the primary handler?
- If both of you are bad at handling money, how will you educate yourselves to get better?
- Do either of you have major credit card debt?
- Do either of you have collections on your credit report?
- Are you going to purchase a house after the wedding?
- Do either of you own a car?
- Are you currently paying an auto loan or are you currently leasing a car?
- How many cars will you have?
- How many children will you have?
- Will they attend private or public school?
- Are you going to save for your children's college education?
- If either of you have a college degree, are there still outstanding loans that need to be paid off?
- Are either of you considering graduate level education? If so, how will you pay for it?
- Are you both satisfied in your careers? Are you satisfied with the salary you make?
- Will you have a joint checking account? If not, why?
- Will you have a joint savings account? If not, why?
- Are you willing to share your earnings with one another?
- How much of your monthly income will be given to the church?

- How will you file your income taxes?
- If you get a refund, what will you do with it?
- Do either of you have a gambling problem? Do either of you habitually play the lottery? If so, are you willing to stop immediately?
- Do either of you have a problem with compulsive or impulsive spending?
- Do either of you have a problem or obsession with shopping?
- How will you buy groceries? Which of you will be responsible for this task or will you share it?
- Who is going to be responsible for paying the bills?
- How will you budget the money you earn?
- Are both of you going to work? If one of you is not going to work, why?
- How much will you spend on entertainment monthly?
- Are you planning on saving a certain amount of money during a specific period for a specific purpose?
- Are you going to invest your money in stocks or CDs?
- Are either of you participating in a 401K plan at your place of employment?
- Do you plan on donating to any charities?
- Where do the two of you see yourself financially in 5 years? 10 years? 20 years?
- How will you honor God with your finances?
- Are you prepared to be forgiving and patient with one another if financial issues arise?
- Will you help one another if either of you run into problems such as a layoff from a job? Will you stand by each other in tough financial times?
- Will you support and encourage each other concerning finances (and possible financial issues)?
- Will you loan each other money, or will you treat the money you both earn as belonging to both of you?
- If one of you makes more than the other, will this be an issue (especially if the female earns more)?
- Finally, are you prepared to work together as a team when it comes to finances?

Wedding Ceremony Financial Questions

- Who is going to finance the wedding ceremony?
- As the bride, are you able to purchase your wedding gown or is someone buying it for you?
- For the groom, have you found an affordable tuxedo rental place for yourself and the groomsmen?
- Are you having a wedding reception? If so, how much will it cost?
  - Are you going to have food catered in or are you going to utilize food from a restaurant or banquet hall?
  - Who is going to purchase the wedding cake?
  - Have you both purchased rings for one another? If you bought them on credit, are they paid off or do you have installment payments left?
  - Are you going to be taken to the reception hall by limousine? If so, who is going to pay for it?
  - Are you going to have a gift registry at a department store or specialty store of your choice?
  - Are you going to have a wedding coordinator?
  - Have you purchased your marriage license?
  - Are you going to give the presiding minister an honorarium?
  - Are you going on a honeymoon? If so, are you paying for it or is someone sponsoring your trip?
  - Do you have spending money for the honeymoon?
  - What is the total spending limit for your wedding and reception?

SESSION SIX

The Wedding Ceremony

Purpose: To go through the actual wedding ceremony to make sure the wedding is successful and special for the bride and groom

The items discussed here are subject to change at your discretion. What I have provided for you in this written session is an outline of a basic wedding ceremony that you can choose to utilize on the day of your wedding. In no way am I suggesting that your ceremony be strictly designed as I have it outlined here. You may have intentions of employing a wedding coordinator who may or may not have different ideas from the ones suggested here. I want the two of you to relax and understand that how the ceremony takes place is up to you. The items listed below are very general in nature and are meant to give you an idea of how a wedding ceremony should flow.

In the appendix, I have provided a wedding sermon that I have previously shared at a wedding that I officiated. That sermon was designed to last twenty minutes. However, it is solely up to you if you would like a sermon portion included in your special day.

1. Initially, the **groom** and the minister will enter and proceed to the front of the church. The groomsmen may also enter the church from the side at this time or they may proceed in with the bridesmaids. The choice is yours. The most important thing at this point is that the **groom** and the person performing the ceremony are in place for the procession of the bridal party and of course, the bride herself.

2. The **parents** (and grandparents, if applicable) of the bride and groom will be escorted to the front pews of the church by the ushers. Background music can be provided at this time to set a calming atmosphere for the ceremony.
3. The **bridal party** will proceed into the sanctuary of the church. You can decide if you want them to enter to silence or be accompanied by music of your choice. Please make sure the music is tasteful and preferably Christian in nature (especially the lyrics). The **bridesmaids** will enter first either alone or accompanied by the **groomsmen**. The **flower girls and ring bearer** will enter at this time.
4. Everyone will be expected to stand as the **bride** enters the sanctuary escorted by her father. The musician can play the traditional bridal march, or another song of your choice can be played in the background. Please be tasteful with whatever you choose.
5. At this time, we will have the **giving of the bride** done by her father. The script will read as follows:
    To Father: *Who gives this bride in marriage?*
    Father's Response: *I do.*
    To groom: *Take your bride and step forward please.*

Ask that the congregation remain standing as we go before the Lord in prayer.

6. At this time, the presiding minister will do a short prayer.
7. The congregation will be told to be seated after the prayer is done.
8. A charge to the Bride and Groom will be given by reading portions of chapter five of Ephesians.
9. Both the bride and groom will be asked if they have accepted Christ in this manner:
    To Groom: *Have you accepted Jesus Christ as your Lord and personal savior?*

Response: *I have.*
To Groom: *Have you received the Holy Spirit to dwell in you?*
Response: *I have.*

To Bride: *Have you accepted Jesus Christ as your Lord and personal savior?*
Response: *I have.*
To Bride: *Have you received the Holy Spirit to dwell in you?*
Response: *I have.*

10. At this time, some brief words are shared pertaining to your salvation and your marriage. Then some words are shared with the congregation regarding marriage. The **sermon** can be inserted here. The length of time will be based on your preference.
11. Proceed with the **Profession of Vows**. You can choose to write your own or repeat some standard vows after the minister. I wrote my own vows the morning of my wedding on October 12, 2014. They are stated clearly at the beginning of this book. I like to challenge couples to write their own vows instead of simply using the standard vows. This exercise will give each person a chance to really look at their investment in the marriage covenant that they are about to enter. In other words, writing your own vows will challenge your thoughts and it will help you "buy in" to the covenant agreement that is involved in marriage. The standard vows will be worded in this manner:

To Groom: *Do you take _____ as your wife, as your own flesh, to love her even as Christ loves the church, to protect her and care for her for the rest of your lives?*
Response: *I do.*
To Groom: *Then turn to her and make this profession of your faith: According to the Word of God, leave my father and my mother and I join myself to you, to be a husband to you. For better or worse, rich, or poor, in sickness and in health. From this moment forward, we shall be one.*

To Bride: *Do you take as your husband, submitting yourself to him as unto the Lord, showing reverence to him as the head of this union for the rest of your lives?*
Response: *I do.*
To Bride: *Then turn to him and make this profession of your faith: According to the Word of God, leave my father and my mother and I join myself to you, to be a wife to you. For better or worse, rich, or poor, in sickness and in health. From this moment forward, we shall be one.*

12. **Presentation of the Rings** At this time, you will exchange rings. This is an example of what may be said:
    To Groom: *May I have the bride's ring, please?*

    Minister shares a short statement concerning the symbolism of the ring.

    To Groom: *Take this ring, place it on her left finger, and say to her: With this ring, I thee wed. It is a token of my love for you and a token of my faith that I release now, in Jesus' name.*

    To Bride: *May I have the groom's ring, please?*

    Minister shares a short statement concerning the symbolism of the ring.

    To Groom: *Take this ring, place it on his left finger, and say to him: With this ring, I thee wed. It is a token of my love for you and a token of my faith that I release now, in Jesus' name.*

13. Unity Candle Lighting – This procedure should be practiced thoroughly at the rehearsal.
14. The minister will then ask the two of you to hold hands and say the following words:

To bride and groom: *Representative of Jesus Christ, before Almighty God and in the name of the Father, of His Son Jesus, and by the power of the Holy Spirit, I now pronounce you one together. You are now husband and wife.*

To groom: *You may now kiss your bride!*

**The two of you will kiss briefly and tastefully! **

To bride and groom: *Please turn and face the congregation.*
To the congregation: *Ladies and gentlemen, I present to you Mr. and Mrs._____.*

15. The two of you will then proceed out the church, followed by the entire bridal party. Once the church is clear, you may choose to have a receiving line in which the guests in the congregation will greet each of you along with the bridal party. After that is done, the sanctuary can be cleared for either pictures or to proceed to the wedding reception.

Gregory L. Payton

FINAL NOTE

By now, you have probably set a wedding date and are making the necessary preparations for your big day. I am honored that you picked up this book as a guide as you make one of the most important steps of your lives. I pray that these six sessions are helpful to you on your marriage journey. If you were committed to digging deep and truly doing the work, then you are well on your way to a lasting union. Knowing that these issues have been addressed and discussed makes me feel confident that the two of you will have a successful marriage. If you ever feel the need to revisit any of the information listed here, do not hesitate to do so. Marriage is like a car; it will require tune-ups and maintenance along the way. I pray that God will richly bless this union and if I can be of any assistance in the future, please feel free to contact me. Thank you for allowing me to share with you what God has shared with me concerning the institution of marriage.

Sincerely,
Rev. Gregory Payton

Gregory L. Payton

APPENDIX

Sermon Title:
The Miracle of Oneness

"Haven't you read," he replied, "that at the beginning the Creator made them male and female, and said for this reason a man will leave his father and mother and be united to his wife, and the two will become one flesh? So, they are no longer two, but one. Therefore, what God has joined together, let man not separate." Matthew 19:4-6 (NIV)

We have gathered here today for an incredibly special purpose. Today, we are going to have the opportunity to witness a miracle. God has ordained this very moment in which each one of us present will witness the union of these two people who stand before me. Today, we are going to witness two individuals becoming one in the eyes of God and before all of us as witnesses. What a privilege it is to witness such a miracle. How blessed we are to be a part of this moment that God ordained to take place.

These two young people have expressed their love for one another, and they have shared their desire to become husband and wife. The two of them have undergone six intense months of pre-marital counseling and they have thoroughly prepared themselves for the road ahead. These two young people are both born again believers and they both realize that this day is a part of God's plan for their lives. They also understand that marriage is an institution that was created by God. The society we live in has no place in dictating how a marriage should function. All of us here have married friends or relatives who may be doing things their way when it comes to marriage. However, we must keep in mind that the originator, or better yet the innovator, of this thing called marriage expects for it to function a certain way. With the divorce rate at an all-time high, it is in our best interest to base our marriages on biblical principles as opposed to carnal practices.

    The bride and groom standing before me both look wonderful. The bridal party and all the participants in this ceremony are all dressed very well. All of you sitting in the congregation look wonderful also. I must say that I don't look so bad myself today! However, we are not here today to put on a theatrical presentation. Everyone here is not simply dressed in a costume that coincides with the role they are playing in this ceremony. We are here, as I stated earlier, to witness a miracle. We are here to witness the oneness of the two people nervously standing before me. I know some of you came to see what the bride had on. I know some of you came to see if the groom was going to show up. I know that some of you may have come to see how the two families would act once they were placed in the same room. Some of you may have simply come out of respect for this couple because you were invited to come. You may be here to simply drop off a gift or card. There may even be some of you present here today simply because you want to eat and have fun at the reception. Well, I have news for all of you. God is the one who made arrangements for you to be here. God ordained this marriage and God orchestrated the circumstances for all of you to be present at this very sacred moment. Two people are about to become one. You are about to witness the oneness of this beautiful young couple become a reality right before your very eyes.

    As we journey back in time to the earthly ministry of Lord and Savior Jesus Christ, we find our Lord amid a rabbinic debate with some pharisees. These men are attempting to test the theological knowledge of our Lord and Savior by asking Him questions that they ignorantly think will trip Him up. They ask is it okay for a man to divorce his wife for any reason he chooses. If any of you were to ask me that same question today, my answer would be similar to the one Jesus gave them in verses four through six of chapter nineteen of The Gospel of Matthew. I don't profess to be as spiritual or as godly as Jesus Christ himself, but I do understand the Word of God.

    Jesus begins His response by quoting a passage of old testament scripture that is familiar to most of us here today. Jesus proceeds by questioning whether the pharisees had heard this scripture before. Sadly, some of here today may have never read this scripture before or any scripture at all. Jesus quotes Genesis 2:24 which states that a man will leave his parents to be united to his wife and they shall become one flesh. The original marriage or the first marriage that God created was verbalized to us through this passage of scripture. God intended for this passage to be read over and over for us to understand what he intended for all married couples. God wants married couples to be one with another or to practice oneness for the remainder of their lives.

This principle of oneness is so counter-cultural to the self-centered society we all live in. After all, we are all individuals who have the freedom to do what we want when we want to do it. We are told throughout life to "look out for number one!" However, when you get married there is no such thing as a number one. As a married couple you will be one. Somehow, we must practice this principle of oneness in our marriage because Satan is going to do everything, he can to make us focus on what we want and what we need instead of what our spouse wants or needs.

As we go back to our text, we discover that our Lord presents this old testament passage with a couple of additional statements of His own to firmly state His position. Jesus states that the husband and wife are no longer two but one. This oneness that we are looking at today applies to every area of your life.

Spiritually, the two of you will be one. Your mindset and focus on how to worship God should be one of unity. Spiritually, both of you as one should strive to grow together as a couple. Each of you should be better people and more spiritually mature through your oneness. You should pray together and read the Bible together. Who better to be prayer partners with than each other? You should serve in ministries together if your gifts are similar. You should support each other in ministry and in other areas of life. If the wife is singing somewhere, the husband should be there cheering his wife on whether she sounds good or not. If the husband is a preacher, the wife should be at every speaking engagement in support of her man. You should both have a mindset that is centered around glorifying God in everything that you do. Your oneness ties deeply into your spirituality and you should not take that fact for granted.

Physically, the two of you will become one. You are to share your bodies only with one another. The physical union of your relationship should be a celebration of your marriage and it should be done in a way that glorifies God. No one outside of your relationship should play any role in your physical oneness.

Socially, you are one. Yes, you may have different interests and personalities. However, now is the time for you to unite socially so that you can enjoy life together. It should no longer be just his friends or her friends, especially if someone in any of these two groups dislikes one of you. There should be mutual friendships. There should be times socially where it is just the two of you. However, there will be times when you are in a group, however everyone present should know that you are husband and wife. You will be one, so act like it. You are making a covenant with each other, not your friends. They should never come first and if you as friends of the bride or groom are here today, know that God will hold you accountable if you allow your friendship with either of these two people to cause tension in their marriage. If friendships outside of the marriage hinder the marriage, cut them off! This is how God would want it. So, don't be mad at the preacher today!

Financially, you are one. It is time for you to share what you earn with one another. If possible, get a joint checking account. Set goals together on how you will handle and save money. In your giving, be united. Neither of you should have secret stashes of money all over town or secret saving accounts for your own interest. I hope you didn't secretly have a prenuptial agreement outside of the premarital counseling. There should be trust among you regarding finances. Be one when it comes to money. Don't let financial insecurity destroy your marriage.

These four things I mentioned are just a snapshot of the many ways that you can function as one in your marital relationship. God has chosen to place the two of you together. How you handle what He has given you determines how much you appreciate the gift of oneness that He has bestowed upon you.

Always use the Bible as your handbook on how to live as a married couple. The Bible will show you how to treat one another. It will show you how to honor and respect one another. Remember, you are going to be one. Don't let other people tell you how to handle your marital problems or issues. I hope those of you in the audience heard what I just said. Always trust in God and seek Him to help and guide you in your marriage. Cling to each other. Depend on each other. Love each other in a way that brings glory to God. Talk to each other. Treat each other the way you want to be treated. You are one. You are no longer two.

To the witnesses here today, I don't want you to feel left out. The bride and groom today appreciate your presence here. You are here to witness this miracle. However, you are also here to receive some instructions on how you will relate to this couple that is getting married today. In the last sentence of our text, Jesus states that what God has joined together, let man not separate. In the context of this verse, man is a generic reference to mankind. Mankind has no right to end or destroy what God has created. I speak today about this issue with the authority of the Bible, not my own opinion. Do not do anything to hinder this union. Interfering would be sinful on your part.

The scripture tells us that God has joined this couple together and we have already established that this moment was **ordained** by God for the purpose of these two becoming one. Your responsibility is to make sure these two remain one! Please don't interfere in their relationship. Please don't be the one to take them away from one another because you are socially lonely yourself. Keep your opinions about their marriage to yourselves. Do not gossip about them. Do not slander their names. If they ask for your advice or help, give it if it is biblical, but don't be a hindrance to them. If your advice is going to be carnal or worldly, keep it to yourself! If you see that one of them is headed in the wrong direction in life, pray for that person. Always remember that you have no right to destroy what God has created. God created the marriage union that is coming into existence today. Who are we to interfere?

Therefore today, I challenge all of you who are under the sound of my voice today to mind your own business. I challenge you to pray for this couple. I challenge you to be kind and supportive of their lives and everything they set their minds out to do. Pray that God will bless this union. Pray that God will bless the children that come forth from this union. Pray that this couple will bring glory and honor to God through their marriage.

Divorce is not an option for this couple. Pray that Satan will not plant that seed in their marriage. By looking at this passage of scripture today, we understand how Jesus responds to questions concerning divorce. We know that God hates divorce. You should hate it also. We are witnessing the miracle of oneness today. God ordained marriage. God created marriage. God ordained and created this union that is taking place today. This is a special day. This is a special moment. The miracle of oneness is about to take place. We were all summoned here to bear witness to this miracle. My prayer is that this oneness will last all the days of their lives. More than that, I pray that the oneness of this couple will be that which God gets all the glory out of.

The bride that stands before me is beautiful. The groom that stands before me today is well groomed and polished in a way that is worthy of the beautiful bride that he is standing next to. The miracle of this union is only minutes away. I pray that all of us appreciate the miracle of oneness that is going to take place before our very eyes. God bless the bride and groom. God bless all of you in the congregation. God, we all say thank you for allowing us to witness this miracle of oneness!

ACKNOWLEDGEMENTS

First and foremost, I would like to thank my Lord and Savior Jesus Christ for loving me, saving me, and calling me to serve the body of Christ through ministry. The gift of being called to officiate weddings is truly an honor and a privilege. Witnessing the miracle that takes place when two souls become one is amazing. Allowing the Holy Spirit to empower a humble servant like me to play an important role in the beginning of the marriage journey is one of the most rewarding tasks of serving in ministry.

I want to thank my amazing and lovely wife, Keyonna for her unconditional love and support on a daily basis. It is an honor to be your husband. You've given the push I needed to be a better man and a better servant, especially throughout the process of my first book becoming a reality. Our first date was at a wedding I officiated at Buckingham Fountain in Chicago several years ago. Having you by my side that day was the beginning of me finding you. I had no idea that you were going to be the wife that God designed especially for me. I'm glad you said "yes" to that date, and on October 12, 2014 when the miracle of our marriage took place.

I thank and praise God for my wonderful mother, Gwendolyn Payton. As I stated in the dedication of this book, witnessing your marriage to my father (Edison Payton) taught my sister, Dr. Tonya Payton-Coleman, and I several lessons that we will never forget. Tonya, I pray that the both of us will make Mommy and Daddy proud in our marriages.

I thank God for my Pastor, Corey B. Brooks, and New Beginnings Church of Chicago. The love and support Keyonna and I have received from Pastor Brooks and our Church family has been tremendous.

Special shout out to the Brothers of the Xi Lambda Chapter of Alpha Phi Alpha Fraternity, Incorporated. Serving as the Chaplain of our Chapter is one of the things that inspired me to be a better wedding officiant. Alpha men are taught to be servants of all. I try to serve with excellence every time I officiate a wedding.

I want to acknowledge the institution where I earned my Master's degree, Moody Bible Institute. This premarital guide actually began as a semester project in my Pastoral Theology class. After earning an "A" on the project, I decided to keep the draft as a pdf that I have shared with several couples before I performed their wedding ceremonies. The positive feedback I received from those couples inspired to get this work published. I am grateful for the encouragement.

The Lord allowed me to cross paths with Sister Kristen Harris at my home church, Logos Baptist Assembly many years ago. I was inspired by her vision to publish the books of aspiring authors. I am grateful for The Scribe Tribe Publishing Group and all of the wisdom and guidance I have received from Kristen. I thank God for your ministry and your courageous vision. Thank you for agreeing to publish this premarital guide.

I want to acknowledge all of the couples whose weddings I have officiated. Thank you for allowing me to be a witness to *The Miracle of Oneness* that took place on your wedding day.

To all of my family and friends, I love and appreciate all of you. To my ministry colleagues and fraternity brothers, thank you for support and inspiration.

I pray that this work will benefit everyone that reads it. I pray that the couples who read this before entering into marriage will be inspired and encouraged to have a marriage that honors God. I pray that married couples will find this helpful as well. I pray that pastors, ministers, and wedding officiants will find this work helpful as you prepare for the task of officiating weddings.

Witnessing *The Miracle of Oneness* that takes place on the wedding day is a joy, honor, and blessing from the Lord. Amen.

ABOUT THE AUTHOR

Reverend Gregory L. Payton is an ordained minister of the Gospel. He is the dedicated and loving husband to Keyonna. He is also a proud father of five (Julian, Justin, Gabrielle, Jayla, and Jayden) and grandfather of Kaydence. This humble servant is a graduate of Moody Bible Institute and a member of Alpha Phi Alpha Fraternity, Incorporated where he serves as chaplain for the Xi Lambda Chapter. He has a passion for preaching, teaching, and serving the body of Christ.

One of his ministry passions is officiating weddings. He is a uniquely experienced wedding officiant. Rev. Payton's goal in ministry is to engage and humbly serve the body of Christ, to lead lost souls to Christ, and to make disciples of Christ. Rev. Payton hopes to accomplish these ministry goals through church planting.

For bookings, please contact him via email at revgp1@gmail.com.

Gregory L. Payton

WORKS CITED

Chapman, Gary. *Toward a Growing Marriage.* 1979, 1996. Moody Press. Chicago, IL 60610.

Elwell, Walter A. *Baker Theological Dictionary of the Bible.* 1996. Baker Books. Grand Rapids, MI 49516-6287.

Goodrick, Edward W. & Kohlenberger, John R. III. *Zondervan N.I.V. Exhaustive Concordance.* 1990, 1999. Zondervan Publishing. Grand Rapids, MI 49530.

LaHaye, Tim, *Why Do You Act The Way You Do?* 1984. Tyndale House Publishers. Wheaton, IL 60189.

The American Heritage Dictionary. 1994. Bantam Doubleday Dell Publishing Group. New York, NY 10036.

The Holy Bible. New International Version. 1996. Zondervan Publishers. Grand Rapids, MI 49530.

www.ingramcontent.com/pod-product-compliance
Lightning Source LLC
Chambersburg PA
CBHW062154100526
44589CB00014B/1830